FINANCIAL LIBERTY

The path way to financial Freedom

Ray Marcel

Content

Chapter 4

Waiting

Chapter 5

Giving

Chapter 6

Gratitude

Dedication

I devote this Book to God Almighty who has given me the insight to Put together this truckload of learning both by experience and by books and to my Wonderful Parents and my beautiful Wife and my Kids and sincerely to the destitute individuals of our world

Preface

It is my expectation and supplication that this book will start a development that will end the frightful measurements of neediness and need in our present reality.

- Could you at any point accept that 80% of individuals in this present reality live on under ten bucks every day?
- Three billion individuals live on two bucks per day, while one billion live on under a dollar daily!
- 50,000 individuals bite the dust day to day due to neediness related causes!

Cash won't make you rich, since it isn't intended to do as such. To be rich is to figure out the importance of cash and abundance and to know the distinction between the two. Cash isn't really abundant, so a great many people who want to be rich are not really searching for cash. What they are really searching for is abundance. Cash just comes to individuals who are now rich or well off in soul and soul, so really not cash makes you rich — you are rich before cash even comes your direction. Cash possibly answers when these components are set up, and until such a period, cash won't move toward you. Cash won't make you rich, in light of the fact that a man who is poor in soul is unfortunate through and through, in any event, when he has a large chunk of change in his pocket. Cash without the abundance of the spirit is risen to a gathering of distresses and laments. Just God improves without adding distress to it. Cash doesn't come to great individuals — on the grounds that there are a huge number of good individuals who aren't rich. Cash doesn't come to taught individuals — on the grounds that there are such countless taught individuals carrying on with working class lives in our present reality. Cash doesn't come to churchgoers or Christians. On the off chance that that were the situation, our holy places would be loaded up with tycoons! Actually, cash isn't guaranteed to come to finance managers, as so many are battling even to earn barely enough to get by. Cash just arrives at the people who are now wealthy in the information on the laws of cash. On the off chance that you are not currently wealthy in your psyche, then, at that point, cash won't come to you. Until you are wealthy to you, you're not rich by any stretch of the imagination.

So what is Riches?

Abundance is the subtotal worth of resources possessed by an individual. The first importance of abundance was: "to have extraordinary characteristics, values and ideals." fundamentally, an individual wishing to be rich is really thinking as far as everything he needs and needs. What, then, is cash? Financial specialists call "lawful delicate," and something is by and large acknowledged for installment, trade, and valuing cash. Cash is what we use to gauge abundance, since it is the simplest method for moving and handling riches. The data in Money Won't Make You Rich starts to have more significance when you check it from the crystal of the previously mentioned definition. You can have abundance without fundamentally having cash, since cash won't make you rich. Then again, you can have cash without being rich, since you really want to initially be affluent, both in resources and temperances, before you can be genuinely rich. Cash is just a piece of handled wood or metal, so it's not worth trading your life for. All things considered, you ought to look first to create the financial wellbeing of both material and inward qualities, and afterward cash will start pursuing you. You should be rich before cash comes to you. Cash truly affects individuals: it is possible that it rules and controls, or it is dominated and constrained by its proprietor. The impact it has on not entirely settled by whether you are first well off in quite a while and ethics. In this book I have tried to impart bits of insight to you that will most likely empower you to turn out to be monetarily free — assuming you will just comply with the laws of cash that are uncovered. All the more significant to me, I need to not just liberate you from destitution and need, yet I additionally need to set you ablaze to turn into an instrument of independence from the rat race to all men any place they are.

Chapter 1

Thinking

As he thinks in his heart, so is he.

The best way to for all time change the temperature in the room is to reset the indoor regulator. Similarly, the best way to change your degree of monetary achievement "forever" is to reset your monetary indoor regulator.

Abundance creation requires a mentality that lessens commercialization and embraces business. The pioneering mentality examined in this book isn't to bump you towards the careful course of beginning a business, however to assist you with grasping the essential association among psyche and riches.

A portion of the focuses here might appear glaringly evident, yet however clear as they seem to be, they are the most minimized. On the off chance that you desire to achieve independence from the rat race in the midst of the worldwide monetary emergency, embrace and apply these different enterprising attitudes in your reserve funds, ventures, projects, and so forth, and remain reliable with each step.

In monetary preparation, you really want the right attitude to win. It doesn't make any difference how much exertion you put in, on the off chance that you are not in the right mood it will be a difficult errand to arrive at your objectives. Cambridge word reference characterizes a mentality as an individual's perspective and their viewpoints. Very much like having the right mentality in life will open entryways for you, having the right outlook will effortlessly sling you to arrive at your speculation objectives quicker.

The right attitude will get you far, and open ways to open doors that you may not in any case access

You are the entirety of what you think a result of what occurs in you, Friends there is something inside you, as you plunk down to quality reflection, with there should be an exit plan disposition, you incite the fortunes on your inside to approach, it's basic to realize that each occasion is a creation and each development is a result of instinct, what is instinct? Only subjective reflection, which is the capacity to beneficially arrange considerations. The reckless child started thinking clearly and found his direction back home by thinking. I don't think it required over an hour of thinking to do that. This is one of the neglected, however most remarkable powers throughout everyday life.

You have a phenomenal soul, all you really want to do is to connect with it. Your vehicle has a stuff framework, however until you connect with the stuff, the vehicle won't move, we should draw in our mindset for triumphs over our monetary life. You get to remember to work, by petition, yet by drawing in thinking, putting current realities on ground and afterward resolving things. Well that is Wisdom!

The level to which you connect with your brain, decide the degree of results you acquire. For example you have a business and it's not flourishing, how about you plunk down and reason, do individuals truly require what I'm selling? In the event that they don't then would it be that they need around here? You have gone to lease an office space in a region, however the administration you are delivering is required in another space. What a disproportionate Wisdom

Nobody constructs a pinnacle without first plunking down to produce, make and examine thoughts, a lot of individuals read strict books which are great, implore and quick to get thriving however not much consideration is given to plunking down to think. For Christains you have abstained and asked now think, thinks just turn out for scholars, Engage imaginative reasoning, for significant level efficiency, I put stock in new things, each new thing emerges from novel insights

Many individuals are a worry to their Creator, This is on the grounds that the things they cry about don't need tears by any stretch of the imagination. They simply require making the proper strides and then strolling into triumph.

In this way of thinking time is the best resource in the school of imagination. A Lot of individuals endure disappointment on account of suppositions. It's smarter to be slow and sure, than to be quick and come up short.

Contemplation is key in thinking things out, what is reflection? It is handling obtained data for quality choices, man should initially reflect i.e think first before he turns into a laborer. Infact thinking, quality reflection is the motor room of a fruitful man, in the event that you should succeed in life you should give the mind something to do.

The possibility of the rich and poor people
To the rich Money is Simple while the unfortunate it's hard

Bringing in cash may not be simple yet it's basic. Money is a result of thoughts, abundance is what you get when you enhance individuals' lives, the more worth you make the more cash you have, it's a trade for administration as a matter of fact the greater the help the greater the check. The unfortunate methodology cash with this hard mindset, no not thus, on the off chance that cash was hard diligent employees would have been the wealthy individuals, it's essentially straightforward and vital.

Figure group to make it while the unfortunate needs to make it single-handedly

It takes a group to create valid and enduring financial momentum, John D Rockefeller during his time had the right arrangement of individuals to work with and this among numerous different things made him the most well off man of current history. In the event that one can pursue a thousand two can pursue 10,000, a three overlay line isn't handily broken. This is the mindset of the rich and that is the reason they continue to get increasingly rich while the poor grieves in need since they want to do it isolated, we as a whole need assistance from somebody some time or another no man alone is a superhuman. In the realm of men you want men to work with you to have the option to leave an imprint and leave text style prints in the sand of time. It's the right arrangement and cooperation that make things work.

Dream about Money while the other stress over cash

Stress adds only tired us down, alot of individuals invest their valuable energy agonizing over what to eat and drink how to get the money to carter for self, they cause fears upon themselves and involving the intellectual capacity the spot of value reasoning starts crying and expectations are as of now not alive. One writes and I quote dreams are not those things we see while we are snoozing they are those things that hold us back from dozing, there is an unmistakable distinction among dream and stress and the two share nothing practically speaking except for are in opposition to one another. Dream keeps alive and gives extraordinary expectation while stress just stifles the soul which supports us.

The unfortunate thinks cash is the base of all abhorrent and negative while the rich know absence of cash is the genuine foundation of insidiousness

With the manner in which individuals see cash you will comprehend the reason why they don't have it. The unfortunate think those with cash are glad, it's completely false that both the rich and the poor are responsible for the existence of pride. What is pride? It is a misjudgment of self and giving its appearance agreeing. They are a lot of destitute individuals who are even more glad than even lords and sovereigns, abundance figuratively speaking does not decide worldliness, nor is it inseparable from it neither neediness an outflow of authenticity, it's basic to take note of that The Almighty God who is the most holiest is likewise the most richest! The unfortunate think cash is answerable for the pessimism in the general public, not its the adoration for Money is exclusively liable for each bad habit in our networks

Figure procedure to bring in cash while the unfortunate thinks screwy ways

Methodology is just a game plan intended to accomplish a long haul or by and large point. A long haul or generally speaking point achieves enduring effect riches.

Five Ways to strategize are

Plan.

Ploy.
Design.
Position.
Point of view.

Four Levels of procedure are;

Corporate level procedure.
Business level procedure.
Utilitarian level system.
Functional level procedure.

So from the above you can see the rich figure his direction as far as possible and the end will represent him

The rich think cash as a safeguard while the unfortunate consider it to be frailty

Nothing presents security like cash, everything replies to cash security comprehensive, the rich consider cash to be a way to have security and thinks it that way and they determine ways of making a greater amount of it, while the unfortunate sees it as turmoil, I can't have all that they let you know where will I put it, on the off chance that the primary spot you can't really hate everything. Needing or thinking to have each belief is as of now illegal of Wealth. Take a gander at the general public you live in. The people who are appropriately directed and safeguarded are the rich no matter what their kind of revenue, nobody truly cares about poor people, they are available to assault and obligated to death free of charge. Cash isn't simply a Currency it's a guard instrument, the wealth nations of the world have the best protection component and safeguard framework relevant to people as well

The unfortunate think wealth as karma

Say thanks to God For Grace! Considerably more say thanks to God for the beauty of Labor. Wealth is no karma, they are the conscious demonstrations of men from frantic personalities seeking frantic outcomes! Take a gander at him. He is just fortunate we began together or I began before him is the song of praise for him that is poor. There is something else to wealth besides what we see, from my meeting with unmistakable money managers, One let me know he works 18 hours consistently and just rest during ends of the week, one more let me know he works 16 hours non-stop! What must others see is the outcomes and they like them sure outcomes are agreeable and they believe is karma. It's more than simple karma in the event that it were karma would you say you are adversely affected by being fortunate?

The unfortunate thinks hard work makes abundance while the rich think on influence

In the event that difficult work is the mystery of independence from the rat race, Construction site laborers would be the wealth individuals, there is something else to life besides hard work, it's vain for you to get up right on time and rest late and eat the bread of agonies

Individuals with influence have a lot of domain over those with less influence, in other

The unfortunate think of saving while the rich think of venture and procuring.

The repercussions of the second rush of the pandemic prompted serious financial slumps. North of 10 million Indians endured employment misfortunes and around 97% of families experienced income misfortunes. Modern creation plunged to normal by 28% in G20 economies inside the space of two months (among February and April 2020). Bigger decays somewhere in the range of 40 and 60% were kept in Indonesia, Italy, South Africa, and India. Minor decays were additionally kept in Korea and Russia. Showing these information and realities isn't for re-opening the scars and deformities that have prompted a worldwide monetary emergency, however to control our brains towards the bearing of business venture and efficiency. Assuming the Covid-19 crude has shown us anything, is that-we can never again depend on our positions for security. And on second thought of being socially designed with the 'customer mentality', we really want to begin embracing an 'pioneering outlook' as a safeguard against the current financial choppiness.

How Does Developing an Entrepreneurial Mindset Relate to Wealth Creation?

For the vast majority, the possibility of maintaining a business or having a tenable speculation can be unnerving and awkward. The justification for this is on the grounds that - most of the general population is still socially customized to 'consume', i.e, consuming labor and products, consuming substance in the type of schooling or amusement, pursuing position, and attempting to get utilized by huge organizations (laid out by business people).

With this sort of buyer mindset, it turns out to be difficult to make riches and kill destitution for a bigger scope. To that end there are more jobless alumni and occupation searchers than there are business visionaries.

Definitely, everybody is a purchaser, yet which isolates the rich from the poor is that the well off or 'effective few' have accomplished that status by moving their brains from 'what might I at any point purchase' to 'what could I at any point make', 'which occupation would it be a good idea for me I apply for' to 'What business could I at any point make so I can have my representatives'.

Valid, it isn't simple making a business or keeping up with it, yet it becomes easy to grasp whenever you've fostered the mental reasoning of a business person, in your everyday way of life, yet by the way you see the social climate and its economy.

It is a presence of mind guideline; the well off stay rich since they give what society and individuals in the public eye consume. Also, on the grounds that they realize that a larger part of individuals are apathetic, and they deteriorate themselves with accepted practices, customs, and doctrine, they (the rich) continue controlling and directing the economy. Some of the time, this sort of control or guideline isn't manipulative or narrow minded, however excellent and practical 100% of the time.

Pioneering Mindsets to Adopt and Sustain

Revoking the buyer attitude is basically the initiation of the pioneering 'mentality shift'. Here are some vital stages to embrace and sustain to finish the interaction.

1. Embracing a Mindset of Abundance

There are two normal outlooks to have-a mentality of 'shortage' and a mentality of 'overflow'. The previous is a cheapening of self and perception, while the last option is an enthusiasm for self and perception. Individuals with a world view limited by fear generally trust that: there are never an adequate number of assets or open doors for them, or they are major areas of strength for not sure enough to take on specific errands, difficulties, or exercises. Due to this sort of mindset, they deteriorate in one position, either pushing ahead or in reverse. They become OK with 'commercialization' in this specific circumstance.

Shockingly, the world view limited by fear isn't just endured by poor people however for the most part by people who bring in a lot of cash from their positions. Individuals who count six figures every year from working a steady employment scarcely think past their positions or past working for individuals. They lounge in the deception of solace, commercialization, and security which contracts their outlook to believe that-"on the off chance that I lose this employment, I become no one worth mentioning" or on the other hand "assuming I lose this employment, I can never again make riches". What's more, to this end they experience monetary issues when they at last lose their positions or resign (even with an investment account).

An outlook of overflow is a mentality of riches. It opens your brain to the conceivable outcomes of how to reinforce your self-esteem, how to make different surges of pay without spending a lot on a task, and how to work on your efficiency. The overflow mentality is a significant part of the enterprising outlook since it incites imagination and successful dynamic in the part of monetary administration

2. Clean Your Creative Mindset

Holding an inventive flow is a basic piece of fostering an enterprising mentality, and it is one of the mystery ingredients to abundance creation. Fellow benefactor of Pixar and previous Disney president-Edwin Catmull once said;

As far as I might be concerned, innovativeness incorporates critical thinking. That is the wide definition

Business people frequently picture an open door, a chance of 'what exists' and 'what could exist', and they make thoughts that can blend both, to give an answer.

An enterprising mentality uses advancement and effective fixes for social, modern, and innovative issues. It is tied in with thinking-"how might I take care of this issue" as opposed to "who, or what can assist me with tackling this issue". The previous is an imaginative outlook for achieving objectives, offering some benefit to other people, and receiving genuine benefit consequently, while the last option is a customer mentality for stagnation and simple endurance.

3. An Open-Mind Combined with Knowledge

An old business mentor of mine, Kenny Nwokoye, acquainted me with the risks of what he called the 'fixed attitude'. He said that people with a decent outlook are pleased and haughty about what they definitely know or put stock in, that they are not ready to learn something else, have confidence in whatever else, or focus profoundly on anything more. Furthermore, individuals with such a mentality can't make riches or develop to be monetarily stable since they are not liberal and are not able to grow their insight on what's conceivable.

Discussing the innovative attitude prior, we saw that a business person inspects 'what exists' and 'what could exist', a similar methodology can be applied here, that is-'what is conceivable' and 'what could be conceivable'. In the event that you are hoping to make and oversee abundance, you ought to constantly be aware of 'what could be conceivable', to empower you to investigate better business choices and monetary open doors.

In any case, applying liberality with knowledge is significant. Robert Greene in a web recording said that being receptive without legitimate information as reinforcement resembles having the psyche of a kid. You must be receptive to information and encounters and furthermore apply them to encourage monetary objectives and goals.

4. Building Consistency

An enterprising outlook requests consistency very much like each and every significant thing throughout everyday life. On the off chance that you wish to make significant abundance you must be intellectually focused in remaining predictable with your arrangements and goals. Try not to permit the heap of decisions and interruptions to influence you from accomplishing your objective. To get more familiar with how to remain steady in a world loaded with decisions see this.

I will discuss Consistency in a forthcoming section of delaying and persistence in abundance creation

In Summary

The journey and want to make abundance is a common goal by individuals from one side of the planet to the other. It is a central need to make riches and be monetarily sound. Curiously, one of the numerous things that different the well off from the other monetary classes is their outlook.

To make riches, it is important to situate yourself with the right temper and disposition that will permit you to work at accomplishing the independence from the rat race you want. In this synopsis I will share a few attempted and tried techniques to assist us with fostering the right abundance making outlook.

How do you have any idea about what your ongoing cash mentality is?

A cash outlook is a superseding disposition that you have about your funds. It drives how you settle on key monetary choices consistently. Furthermore, it can hugely affect your capacity to accomplish your objectives. In the event that you alter your outlook about cash, you will quite often settle on better decisions about how to beat difficulties. For this situation, the force of positive reasoning truly matters.

In fostering the right attitude to make riches, it means quite a bit to understand what your ongoing mentality is. This information will help you in understanding what your attitude is and how you really want to further develop it. It is exceptionally fascinating what the seemingly insignificant details you don't consider can mean for and influence the manner in which you think about riches and cash. Things like your experience growing up, how your folks discussed cash around you, your current circumstance, the sort of companions you have, your schooling and even notice that you are presented to. Everything assumes a part of your mentality. Tragically, we don't respite to contemplate why we act the manner in which we do.

Once more, when you consider the rich, what rings a bell? Do you think this is essentially difficult to accomplish? or then again you inquire: "how could they make it?" While others think cash is malicious and thus it is fine to have barely enough for the afternoon, others drive themselves to have more to make an effect. Posing yourself these inquiries gives you a thought about where you are at present. Keep in mind, as a man suspects, he is as well. You can't make more than you suspect - assuming you think little, little is what you are born with.

What is the best outlook for abundance creation?

In the event that speculation little births little, surely dreaming large would be better. An outlook that makes abundance should initially accept abundance creation is conceivable and can be accomplished regardless of your present status. Be aggressive in your fantasies and goals. Ignore any perceived limitations and dream greater in light of the fact that the world is brimming with potential outcomes and the open doors exist.

I can nearly hear you say: "I thought beyond practical boundaries but fizzled every step of the way and with each open door came my direction." Well then I suppose you share a comparable story with one of the world's most extravagant men, Jeff Bezos and numerous others. Jeff Bezos said: "That's what I knew whether I fizzled, I would love that, however I knew the one thing I could lament isn't attempting". An outlook that makes abundance doesn't dread to flop however just feelings of trepidation not attempting by any stretch of the imagination.

Demoralization and disappointment are two of the surest venturing stones to progress as per Dale Carnegie, exhorting that we foster accomplishment from disappointments. Many individuals dread these two. On the off chance that you start to see disappointment as a stepping stone, you have the right mentality. Assuming that you start to view disappointment as giving you that push or inspiration, then you are having an outlook shift that is carrying you closer to making riches.

You want to develop your cash or better actually give your cash something to do to make abundance. Putting some cash to the side is an incredible beginning, but your cash needs to work for you. There is risk in giving your cash something to do. It's relatively more secure to set aside your cash in a cash drawer at home or a ledger. Be that as it may, you will not make abundance by just saving and not facing any challenge whatsoever. An abundance creation mentality faces some challenges, and without a doubt what is agreeable.

A ton of times we assume we are either excessively youthful or too old to even consider effective money management, yet that is never the situation. You are never excessively youthful or excessively old to begin making riches. Walt Disney the proprietor of the popular Disneyland said: "The method for getting everything rolling is to stop talking and start doing." A mentality that successes at abundance creation, is one that absolutely makes it happen. Indeed, the reasons sound great, be that as it may, assuming it is vital to you, John Decker says you will track down a way and not a reason. Try not to hang tight for inspiration - I'm informed it's misrepresented, and it could take excessively lengthy or never come. Still up in the air to bring in cash and do what needs to be done.

Fostering the right outlook

The ideal attitude is positive. Encircle yourself with positive-disapproved individuals and at last, you will foster a comparative mentality. It is said, assuming that you stroll with the astute, you increment their number, along these lines when you stroll with the individuals who have the right outlook, you foster one over the long haul. You at last become like the five-nearest individuals in your circle so pick well.

Fabricate a steady outlook, not one that begins and stops midway. Abundance is made after some time with consistency, so ensure something you fabricate is consistent. Doing easily overlooked details everyday forms a propensity which develops into a way of life, and you will be flabbergasted in a couple of years about what you will have achieved. Holding back to get going large might in all likelihood never happen-start by making a little stride everyday to arrive at your objective!

An inquisitive brain is a learning mind. To make riches, you want to continue learning and posing the right inquiries. Fostering an inquisitive outlook sets you off to making riches. Be interested about the people who have made riches, read about how they came into abundance, pose inquiries on how you can likewise begin making abundance and with time it would work out.

Having speculation conversations with our kids quite early in life is significant. As you foster an abundance creation outlook, convey them along. This is the means by which you foster the right attitude towards abundance creation. You put forth your objective, make the important enquiries and work towards accomplishing your objective.

Chapter 2

Working

Your work is your worth
Our Attitude determines our Altitude

"Success isn't always about greatness. It's about consistency. Consistent hard work leads to success. Greatness will come" according to Dwayne Johnson.

At the point when No one is conceived poor, nor is any one conceived rich. No body was brought into the world with a three-piece of suits and endlessly coordinates of shoes on. Everyone arrived at this world unmistakably bare. Nobody conveyed a satchel or really took a look at the book, when he was conceived. Individuals become anything they decide to be, Sloth makes you poor; ingenuity brings riches. All together words he becomes unfortunate with arrangements with slack hands: the word here is he becomes poor… . Very much like men become rich, others additionally become poor, your decision figures out what you become, yet the hand of the persevering makes them rich, so the creation of abundance isn't restricted to thinking alone, working open the channels of the progression of resources as we probably are aware abundance or flourishing is a trade for your Service, No help no Money.

He sacred writing expresses out loud whatever so ever he does it will succeed, Our maker favors crafted by our hands, believed are great however we need to leave the planning phase and go into the work room, this is where Giants are made, when God made man the unmistakable thing he gave him was work: God took the Man and put him down in the Garden of Eden to till the fields and keep it all together; to till the fields and keep it all together, there's a lot of disorderliness in individuals' resides that is the primary explanation they are poor, regardless of the disclosures and thought and methodologies you have you should figure out it, things just work for laborers, systems just talk toward the end, so you really want eager quest for your Visions and thought all together not to come up short toward the end.

They are excesses of Get-rich-fast colleagues today and they are the speediest to disappointment. Numerous I surmise might take a gander at me and once or the other and shared with themselves, "Mmm, Rey is Lucky." No, Rey is Worky, say thanks to God for Grace however say thanks to God something else for the elegance to Labor. Many individuals are trusting that others will come give them some give, you can never be affluent like that. One of the Victims of absence of work are the Christians they imagine that their salvation rescues them from work, no it doesn't. Your Scripture portrays the maker as a specialist and a mastermind, it takes quality ideas to make the blueprint of the universe and intentional work to carry it to the real world!

The main explanation the vast majority don't get what they need is that they don't have the foggiest idea what they need, you will be paid in direct extent for the worth you make in working in the commercial center, in the mystery of the mogul mind he stated "How you do anything is the means by which you do everything"

Work is an action including mental or actual exertion done to accomplish a reason or result.

Ask ten individuals how the rich got rich and you will hear somewhere around ten thoughts. A portion of the more normal suspicions are that individuals become rich by acquiring fortunes, exploiting those less lucky, or "playing" the financial exchange. I even recollect one government worker who demanded anybody who acquired abundance needed to do so wrongfully.

While a couple of individuals become wealthy in these ways, they are the exemption as opposed to the standard. A review by the Spectrem Group requested 132,000 individuals with a total assets of more than $25 million where their abundance came from. Here are the outcomes:

1. Difficult Work, 87%. The larger part got their abundance by really buckling down. Most tycoons put in extended periods of time, frequently in professions they love enough so that work becomes play.

2. Schooling, 78%. Surely, individuals with school training procure more than those without. Nonetheless, the right kind of schooling for creating financial wellbeing may not be tracked down in a school educational plan. For instance, I know one individual with no advanced education who took what could be compared to 75 credit long stretches of land schooling and amassed enormous land possessions.

3. Savvy Investing, 72%. Try not to mistake savvy effective financial planning for complex speculations. It's simply not that hard for business sectors to contribute shrewdly: begin youthful, contribute consistently, don't conjecture, enhance your speculations over various resource classes and different protections, diminish expenses and limit burdens, and don't time the.

4. Facing Challenges, 63%. I would add, "savvy gambles." Actions like beginning a business, becoming involved with your employer, migrating your family to a city with more brilliant possibilities, evolving professions, or getting to buy speculation land all convey with them a specific level of hazard. What's more, with risk definitely comes disappointment. In The Millionaire Next Door, Thomas J. Stanley and William D. Danko bring up that the normal mogul makes 3.1 major monetary, profession, or business setbacks in a lifetime, while the typical non-tycoon commits 1.6 such errors.

5. Moderation, 59%. I've frequently called this the shared factor of individuals that have riches. My conjecture is that it didn't rank higher simply because numerous developers don't see themselves as parsimonious. They tend to not have composed financial plans, they don't shop at secondhand shops, they purchase name brands, and they spend all that in their financial records. In any case, what they neglect is that they pay themselves first, which incorporates taking care of every one of their bills and expenses, spending vigorously for training, and contributing 20 to half of their check. Then, at that point, they blow what's left. I call that moderation.

6. Being in the Right Place with impeccable timing, 56%; and

7. Karma, 53%. Obviously conditions and karma — factors like timing, knowing individuals who can help you, and being honored with capacities and great wellbeing — assume parts in creating financial stability. What additionally matters,

nonetheless, is being ready to exploit good conditions.

8. Maintaining a Business, 46%. This fits intimately with reason number one: buckling down. At the point when you try sincerely and face savvy challenges in your own business, you go past procuring significant compensation. You construct a significant resource.

9. Direction of an Adviser, 35%. Some portion of reason number three, brilliant financial planning, is being savvy to the point of gaining from gifted tutors and counselors.

10. Legacy, 30%. Indeed, legacy is one wellspring of riches. I'd propose that the greater part of the inheritors who can keep and expand on that abundance do so in view of elements like difficult work, training, and shrewd financial planning.

Apparently the outcome in creating financial momentum is like progress in different regions:

the harder and more brilliant you work, the more achievement you are probably going to have.

In every one of these outcomes one thing is extremely Common, Work! karma itself requires work! Indeed take for instance being at the perfect locations with flawless timing requires exertion, Inheritance also requires aggregate exertion, savvy venture requires the utilization of the mind; cerebrum work, Running a business requires work as well. Vision without energy is a simple deception, dreams and great contemplations of turning into a mogul, the tycoon outlook is generally excellent anyway this can materialize with the drive force instrument of work. The work environment stays hallowed assuming abundance is the necessary result.

Key arranged work makes one a goliath in the race of life.

Chapter 3

Trusting

The subsequent stage to getting favored is trusting. We have laid out the spot of working and the spot of reasoning. Presently we should establish the spot of success in the school of thriving.

A lot have faith in their viewpoints and difficult work yet not many trust the cycle, what upgrades a fruitful lively and working life is confiding all the while. It makes for a beneficial giving.

The people who trust are absolutely reliant upon the cycle, it's one thing to think and something else to work but more vital to trust the interaction, trust achieves the loosen up State of the undertaking and the result of each and every extraordinary experience.

The main way not to take thought forever, is to believe that is your interstate to the domain of thriving, there are such countless individuals who are given to thought, they think and envision incredible things yet never trust the very things they envision, Vision the psychological image representing things to come is just a deception without an energy and a trust for the interaction.

Trust is in various levels

The God kind of trust

God make riches
First you really want to trust God to empower you to realize your contemplations, the sacred texts saying favored is the man that confidence in the ruler and whose trust the master is, Cursed is the man that confided in man and maketh tissue his arm and whose heart departeth from

the ruler, they that confidence in the ruler will be as mount Zion, which can't be moved, however abideth for ever as the mountains are circuitous Jerusalem so the ruler is circuitous his kin from hereafter in any event, for ever

To appreciate genuine thriving, you need to partake in the secret of confiding in God. One thing that effectively orders individuals' trust is cash. Many individuals' spirit and heart is drained to and moored on their cash, God doesn't bring duplication of the method of such individuals, since it will prompt their annihilation. The second your trust is in cash, God pulls it out to a level where you will continue to trust God for each dinner. "He that confidence in his wealth will fall: yet the honest will thrive as a branch.

At the point when cash decides your countenance, it shows that that is where your trust is, I trust God, Money is Crazy, there's nothing in it. You want to trust the wellspring of the Money to have the option to order it. God is the wellspring of Wealth. "What's more, you will recall the ruler thy God since he empowers you to get abundance" so there is the influence you get riches and just given by God who owns the whole world, the earth is the master and its completion.

There is not a viable replacement for trust in the school of flourishing success that is generational. In the event that it should be generational, you should trust God. On the off chance that you can't believe him for provisions, He can't entrust you with his arrangement. The explanation that individuals play monetary tricks, is on the grounds that they can't confide in God to address their issues.

Lets see Davids mysterious

The LORD hear thee in the day of trouble;
The name of the God of Jacob defend thee;
Send thee help from the sanctuary, And strengthen thee out of Zion;

Remember all thy offerings, And accept thy burnt sacrifice; Selah.
Grant thee according to thine own heart, And fulfill all thy counsel.
We will rejoice in thy salvation, and in the name of our God we will set up our banners: The LORD fulfill all thy petitions.
Now know I that the LORD saveth his anointed; He will hear him from his holy heaven With the saving strength of his right hand.
Some trust in chariots, and some in horses: But we will remember the name of the LORD our God.
They are brought down and fallen: But we are risen, and stand upright.
Save, LORD: Let the king hear us when we call.
Psalm 20:1-9 KJV

Trust is an expression of commitment the hebrew boys said

If it be so, our God whom we serve is able to deliver us from the burning fiery furnace, and he will deliver us out of thine hand, O king. But if not, be it known unto thee, O king, that we will not serve thy gods, nor worship the golden image which thou hast set up.
Daniel 3:17-18 KJV

Companions we are not a legally binding relationship with God, but rather in a Son Father relationship with Him.Trusting gets you fulfilled in starvation.

The Self Kind of trust

It is great to confide in God yet on the off chance that you don't have faith in your own self you could not make it at any point out of life. Each one out there becoming wildly successful time trusts their approaches to the top.

There is this article I saw some place

Each one is a visionary, it's great to design your work and working your plans is better
Dreams materialize, just for the individuals who go through their fantasies, life is a fantasy
Vision without enthusiasm is deception I have a reasonable Vision and I'm energetic with a Unique Style
If unwavering mindsets always win in the end I will be quick and consistent to mentor the Winners
I trust in MYSELF and I have confidence in my GOD

Trust some say is a weight yet there is no more weight than carrying on with an existence without trust for anything! How far you go in life is because of how well you can think and trust the cycle. That is where the increment comes in.

The People's Kind of trust

It's currently challenging to confide in the planet we live in light of the fact that a lot of individuals influence the trust of individuals to make things out for themselves, and they fall survivors of double crossers and executioners.

The spot of reasoning is extremely basic prior to trusting and keeping in mind that believing it ought to be finished in a verbalized manner. Thinking precedes trusting, investigating the work that should be finished, the techniques within reach and the successful way the entire way to completion is goal and key to keep away from disappointment

In the Journey of life trust is unavoidable, trust is one of the significant parts or components of life, down to the sit we sit on trust makee it that way life is about endlessly trust is one significant component of Wealth creation an underpinning of flourishing is riches.

You really want to work with individuals and in the event that you have little to no faith in them you can't give them your entirety

Chapter 4

Waiting

Patience is a cornerstone of billionaire Warren Buffett's investment strategy.

Individuals who become well off are the people who stay focused on the cycle and methods engaged with accomplishing their objectives. This is certainly not a sheer persuasive discourse, this is a fundamental standard of business and a standard of life.

At the gamble of sounding gracefully buzzword: Rome wasn't underlying a day, and the equivalent goes for your total assets.

"This appears glaringly evident, yet there are a lot of individuals who possibly center around two things with regards to cash: making it and spending it," Katie Brewer, a CFP and the pioneer behind monetary arranging firm Your Richest Life, wrote in a blog entry. "In any case, that is a transient perspective on cash that doesn't prompt riches."

Zeroing in on expanding your pay is important, certainly, however those profits won't prompt enduring abundance without smart preparation and the persistence to own it.

Look no farther than Warren Buffett. The tycoon CEO of Berkshire Hathaway looks at persistence as a foundation of his triumphant speculation methodology. Buffett over and again encourages individual financial backers to stay consistent in any event, when markets go haywire.

"Financial backers who keep away from high and superfluous expenses and basically sit for a lengthy period with an assortment of enormous, safely funded American organizations will more likely than not get along admirably," he wrote in his 2016 letter to investors.

There's an explanation counsel like Buffett's is pervasive, Brewer said: It works. "Save a part of each and every dollar you procure. Try not to spend more than you have. Make ventures that will bring in your cash over the long run. The vital fixing in every one of those means is persistence," she composed.

Monetary organizers recommend making saving simpler via computerizing commitments to a high return investment fund or retirement account. Saving off the top powers consistency and almost guarantees your abundance will continue to develop.

With regards to financial planning, specialists suggest minimal expense file reserves, a Buffett #1. File reserves are a sort of latent speculation that opens financial backers to an expansive determination of stocks to differentiate and at last limit risk. They're minimal expense and routinely beat effectively oversaw reserves — for however long you're patient.

As Buffett put it, "Nothing bad can be said about getting rich gradually."

What is normal in the venture techniques of fruitful financial backers like Benjamin Graham, Warren Buffet, Christopher Davis, and numerous others?

Examine a portion of the statements of these well known financial backers and you will sort it out...

"The most effective way to quantify your money management achievement isn't by whether you're beating the market, but by whether you've set up a monetary arrangement and a social discipline that are probably going to get you where you need to go." - Benjamin Graham

"A 10% decrease in the market is genuinely normal - it occurs about one time per year. Financial backers who understand this are less inclined to sell in a frenzy, and bound to remain contributed, profiting from the growing long term financial stability force of stocks." - Christopher Davis

"A market slump doesn't irritate us. It is a chance to build our responsibility for organizations with incredible administration at great costs." - Warren Buffett

The feature is that these financial backers put stock in typical ideals that assuming you've chosen the right speculations, 'you will continuously be compensated for your understanding.'

The persistence expected for effective money management is an imperative piece of monetary discipline and demonstrates the way that well you can really take a look at your profound state, insatiability, and oversee cash to accomplish your objectives.

Showing restraint toward your speculation implies that whenever you have chosen the resource to put resources into, you ought not be annoyed by momentary unpredictability in the worth of the venture and remain contributed for the long haul. The thought here is to choose commendable resources at a sensibly decent cost.

Attempting to time the market is a useless activity. You might miss out on an appealing venture, an open door on the off chance that you continue to trust that the cost will arrive at the base. Do take note of that regardless of whether the speculation is accessible at a more exorbitant cost, it might in any case merit purchasing assuming that it has the possible worth to become higher later on.

As a matter of fact, on the off chance that you follow a trained methodology and contribute consistently, it will make timing the market unimportant as your expense midpoints after some time and the advantage of intensifying expands your riches.

It isn't workable for anybody, even the notable financial backers, to precisely anticipate the ideal opportunity to enter or leave the market. The procedure that they follow and the one which wc as a whole should follow is straightforward:

Formulate a technique

Select resources after cautious assessment

Hold them for long haul

Here is a great representation to demonstrate the way that persistence can make all the difference for your ventures:

In 1973, Warren Buffet bought portions of The Washington Post Company for US $10.6 million. After a year, the stock costs plunged almost 20% and it required three years for the stock to develop past Buffet's underlying price tag. Notwithstanding, post that, Washington Post's costs continued to increment as the business figured out how to develop significantly thus did the worth of Buffet's property in the organization. Smorgasbord's interest in the organization is viewed as perhaps of his generally productive one.

Had Buffet reclaimed his venture when the stock costs began falling, he would have endured misfortunes on the price tag, yet in addition missed out on the future development of the stocks. This fruitful speculation can be credited to his conviction that the securities exchange is a gadget for moving the cash from the eager to the patient.

Not every person can dominate the righteousness of tolerance. Be that as it may, it is a significant one for fruitful financial backers to teach since zeroing in a lot of momentary additions can thwart your advancement towards winning long haul objectives.

At the point when you put resources into a road, stocks or common assets, remember that it requires investment for any business to develop and produce benefits. Hence, it wouldn't be shrewd to be messed with what occurs temporarily, insofar as you've settled on the right speculation choice.

Think about this, regardless of whether you have a shared asset arrangement of painstakingly chosen value subsidizes like huge cap reserves, multi-cap reserves, little cap reserves and mid-cap assets, on occasion outside elements might say something regarding the exhibition of the general portfolio. The whole market might be going through a bear stage because of feeble large scale financial or different variables. Thus, your value related instruments might give lower returns during that stage.

At such critical times vital that you frenzy and pursue no rushed choices. Assuming that you have chosen research-supported resources, your speculations will defeat this low stage and produce further developed returns over the long haul. Meanwhile, your non-value speculations will give soundness to your portfolio.

However long haul holding of ventures is significant, it would be impulsive to simply purchase and just drop it. You want to survey your portfolio something like once per year to follow the presentation of your ventures. The survey will empower you to see whether you ought to go on with the speculations or on the other hand on the off chance that there is a need to get rid of any non-performing ones.

Since monetary obligations are least at your age, you ought to zero in on growing a strong financial foundation. Being only 22, value is a magnificent vehicle for you. Yet, the watchword here is tolerance.

The way to win in values is to put it routinely and remain in for the long stretch. In the event that you put away Rs 5,000 consistently throughout the following 30 years at a pace of 11% per annum, you will have Rs 1 crore when you are 52. That is the enchantment of getting time to work for you.

Yet, you want to save each and every month and become familiar with the discipline of not being bothered by market costs. The most effective way to do this is by beginning with a Systematic Investment Plan (SIP) in a common asset where a decent sum consistently goes into an asset of your decision.

Since you are simply beginning, a fair asset would be the best method for kicking start the interaction. These assets have extensive interests in the red and, consequently, are less forceful than unadulterated value arranged common assets. Pick any top performing common asset like HDFC Prudence, DSPML Balanced or Tata Balanced. When you are alright with the dangers related with common asset contributing, you can wander in unadulterated value shared reserves.

After this search for some protection. Since protection isn't a speculation, one needs to assess the protection needs on a case-to-case premise. On the off chance that you have no wards right now, what are you purchasing protection for? In the event that you do and are quick to get guaranteed, choose an unadulterated term strategy.

Recollect to not succumb to plans offering simple/easy gains. Obviously characterize your short, medium, and long haul objectives and afterward select the proper resources in light of your gamble profile and time skyline to objective. Contribute routinely paying little mind to economic situations to develop your riches and accomplish your venture goals.

Term protection is the most basic and most perfect type of extra security. Suppose you take a term protection front of Rs 5 lakh for quite a long time. Would it be advisable for you to bite the dust during this time, the recipient (individual you name in the strategy) gets Rs 5 lakh. Would it be a good idea for you to live, nobody gets anything and you lose the charges.

Yet, at your age, this would cost you a pitiful Rs 1,200 for each annum.

The unavoidable

Think charges. Think Section 80C. This part of the Income Tax Act offers a derivation from available pay. Assuming you put up to Rs 1 lakh in the pertinent instruments determined under this part, you save charge up to that sum.

First you really want to check in the event that your boss offers an opportune asset. In the event that indeed, a level of your essential compensation (12% to be exact) is deducted by your boss towards the Employee Provident Fund (EPF). Since this is done consequently, you want to look at your compensation slip to track down that sum.

Since you are thinking about an extra security strategy, the exceptional you pay is likewise qualified for derivation under Section 80C. So absolute these two figures and see by the amount you setback of the Rs 1 lakh limit.If you actually need to contribute to save charge, then, at that point, you can consider five-year bank fixed stores, the National Savings Certificate (NSC) or the Public Provident Fund (PPF). Every one of these are fixed return instruments with a development of five, six and 15 years separately. Charge saving obligations of various developments are likewise brought out by monetary establishments now and again.

At your age, you should consider Equity Linked Savings Schemes (ELSS). These are expanded value finances that offer a tax reduction under Section 80C. The lock-in period is only three years.

Other than having the most reduced security in period and the capacity to produce the best yield among other duty saving instruments, these assets are likewise more assessment effective. You pay no expense on development. Yet, premium acquired on other fixed-personal assessment saving instruments is burdened. The

PPF is an exemption, yet that could change from now on.

Assuming that you wish to choose an ELSS, look over Value Research's five-or four-star appraised reserves like SBI Magnum Tax Gain, HDFC Tax Saver, Sundaram Tax Saver or Franklin India Tax Shield

As a financial backer, today you are spoiled for decisions. Decisions with regards to which resource class to contribute, through whom to contribute, which administrations to pick and the amount to dispense. Add to it , you likewise have news channels, virtual entertainment stages — all of which give data, information and updates nonstop. Does this currently make your effective financial planning process simple or troublesome? The most recent year and a half has added to the quick expansion in options. All in all, has these made you a superior financial backer or made your effective money management process more proficient? The solution to that is: depends.

Assuming you take a gander at the development of common subsidies in India, putting resources into huge cap, multi-cap, mid-cap , little cap , half and half plans were all suitable in different structures. Throughout the course of recent years, the categorisation has been made more straightforward to empower financial backers to go with ideal choices. This move has assisted the financial backers with distributing the assets in a more proficient way, contingent upon the gamble craving.

Other than the area explicit assets, presently there are geographic explicit assets, which permit you as a financial backer to worldwide partake in speculation choices. This is again a welcome move. The venture interaction and strategies should be easy to comprehend and simple to execute in view of the effective financial planning needs.

For a novice financial backer, who has as of late begun procuring a pay and needs to save a specific piece of the pay for ventures, this can confound. With such a lot of information and data accessible, choice loss of motion creeps in and thus can prompt a poor speculation choice.

For this situation, the most recent trend or most recent return can well impact the planned financial backer to settle on a choice which need not be the right venture decision. An effective financial backer need not have the most elevated IQ (Intelligent Quotient) , however having persistence and an interaction is an unquestionable requirement

The main section a financial backer necessities to do is know thyself. As a financial backer, you want to understand what really matters to you; as in:

Might it be said that you are inclined to take a gander at cost developments consistently and do you get a kick out of the chance to encash the benefits at standard stretches?

How might sharp developments in costs influence your point of view?

Could you at any point sit on cost confusion in stocks for a period which can be a couple of days just or can go up to a couple of months?

The above is just a characteristic rundown. The highlight note is that as a financial backer it is your Emotional Quotient (EQ) which will drive your speculation return. Over and over, it has been seen that steady trade in a record doesn't help financial backers much. The exchange cost gobbles up a significant part of the increases. The advantage of force of intensifying builds just over a more extended timeframe.

One ought not be mistaken for movement and activity. A latency is additionally an activity up to one is clear with respect to why one is idle. Abundance creation is a long distance race and not a run. Begin early and little, whenever required, yet begin.

Chapter 5

Giving

The manner in which God flourishes is unique in relation to the way the world succeeds. What the world calls thriving is the amount you possess; yet in the Kingdom of God, still up in the air by the amount you give, No matter how scrumptious the food you have eaten might be, there's a greatest number of hours it ought to remain in your stomach. After that period, it becomes noxious to your body. We live in the reality where each residing thing adds to remain alive, plants for instance give out Oxygen for other residing things so it can remain alive while people and different species give out Carbon dioxide to stay alive, on the off chance that the plant will not give out Oxygen it's headed to elimination same vein with creatures, so residing is as a consequences of joint commitments of both residing things and non residing things.

Giving is living similarly as breathing is living, the day you quit allowing is the day you begin biting the dust, Nothing is more fulfilling than giving of yourself. It implies you live for more than your necessities and needs. Recall how you have been reminded of times without numbers, that sharing is mindful. Also, it is extremely obvious. It is in our unselfish demonstration of giving that we are situated to get. Be that as it may, don't give a compensation outlook. Give since you are sufficiently honored to share. Be a provider who gives constantly, out of the little you have and out of the overflow you might insight. Giving doesn't just connect with cash. It incorporates giving of your time.

For example, giving of your time could mean sharing your mastery for nothing by giving discussions to understudies on vocation choices, giving your skill to your neighborhood church for an impending task, visiting a kids'/the old individuals' home, and simply investing energy with them.

Giving can likewise incorporate giving tangibly; we presumably have outfits in our storage rooms that are looking great, yet we never again use, give those out.

Indirectly, I am saying everyone has something they can give!
One of the major standards of abundance creation is to give. Tragically not many individuals grasp this guideline and spend their lives contending and getting to succeed. Book of scriptures says give thus will you get however a large portion of us neglect to focus on this basic exhort in our battle for endurance.

Scarcely any months back I read a book by a bookkeeper who had many significant clients. This bookkeeper kept a fastidious record of individuals who provided for a noble cause and the people who didn't. Amazingly he found that every one of the individuals who added to the good cause showed improvement over others. My experience has been comparative. Whenever I had the liberality to give I was compensated multiple times over. What's more, at whatever point I turned out to be stingy I endured. The motivation to give places you in contact with the most awesome aspect of yourself and the entire universe plans to take care of you.

Pitanjali, the incomparable Indian scholar, talked about a similar rule when he propounded his hypothesis that each movement in this universe is round. The earth and planets circle the sun. The earth turns around its hub. Downpour water tumbles to the earth, structures into streams and streams that stream towards the ocean just to rise by and by as mists and downpour. The tree ascends from the earth and after its productive life returns to the earth. All that in nature moves all around and returns to us. Likewise when we have great ideas and sentiments about others they return to us in a type of untold love. At the point when we give cash and help other people we position ourselves to get incredible abundance and wealth. This is the law of nature which not many understand. Ask Bill Gates and Warren Buffet and they will attest this hypothesis. They are truth be told living instances of making abundance through giving.

What can one give? Is it just cash? No we can give our grasping, our work, our
love and information. There is no limit to what we can give. For instance, it's undeniably true that clients in reality simply love getting something free of charge. The equivalent goes in the virtual world. Assuming that you are a site proprietor or website admin, give your guests something thoroughly free and you can wager that they will see the value in your signal. What is the most significant thing that you can provide for your guests free of charge? The inquiry might sound hard yet the response is exceptionally basic - INFORMATION! Throughout the entire existence of humankind, our period has been classified "the data age", definitively in light of the fact that data has

become fundamental to our regular routines. So when you give your clients data, you are, as a result, giving them something really important nowadays. This is only one model. You can track down multitudinous chances to give in your nearby climate.

Never under any circumstance offer with the possibility of getting something as a trade off or making the recipient reliant upon you. Continuously provide for help other people to strengthen themselves and stand on their own feet. Take part in their development. Never at any point let them fill in your shadow. This can be the best endowment of all.

Whenever I was searching for a business opportunity I took a gander at consolidating this extraordinary guideline of abundance creation. I found that this standard worked best with network showcasing. The rationale might be to make abundance for yourself yet you can not prevail until you help other people to succeed. You need to share your insight, exertion, time and guarantee the outcome of others to prevail around here. In network promotion there is no contest like in an ordinary business. You need to partake in the development of your colleagues to succeed. Each fruitful organization advertiser consolidates this standard. This is the explanation: I love network advertising. It is a plan of action where you can succeed provided that you help other people to succeed. It consolidates the rule of giving. A great many people bomb in network market when they disregard this fundamental rule.

To make abundance is to give. Give constantly regardless of whether you have close to nothing. This is the incredible guideline of life. Demonstration of giving extends your spirit and brain. Simply give and watch the entire universe plan to make you rich.

There is a typical confusion that to get rich you must be parsimonious, and not be extremely giving.

In all actuality, it doesn't work that way, liberal individuals will quite often be more prosperous. The explanation? Providing for others makes you less childish, and less narrow minded individuals have all the more a propensity to improve in the two connections and in establishing a strong financial foundation.

Holding cash with an open hand could appear to abuse sound judgment. That's what we feel on the off chance that we don't hang on firmly to our cash and our connections, they will get away. I'm not saying in a real sense hold your cash with an open hand - it addresses our disposition toward cash. At the point when you give, you open yourself up. You permit the dollars to pass on and the opportunity to enter.

Giving works since it is in your own outline to be a provider, and you release beneficial things in your day to day existence that you won't ever see until you get familiar with the craft of unselfish giving. Giving lifts us out of ourselves; we take our eyes off our privileges, our concerns, and our stuff. The new view gives us re-established vision and trust. Giving is strong. - Dave Ramsey

There are men who gain from their abundance just the apprehension about losing it. - Antoine Riverolli

Surplus abundance is a consecrated trust to be overseen to bring about some benefit for other people. - Andrew Carnegie

While you're giving, you don't necessarily in every case need to hold on until you're monetarily secure in light of the fact that giving doesn't need to be connected with cash. There are a ton of ways you can give of yourself and your time that are similarly significant. Here are a few different ways that you can give, both with cash, and without!

- Assist a single parent with purchasing food or cover two or three bills.

- Volunteer time at your congregation serving others.
- Give a super huge tip to a server or server.
- Invest energy with individuals at a neighborhood nursing home, talking and paying attention to them, playing music for them or simply messing around with them.
- Pay for somebody's feast behind you in line at the drive-thru eatery.
- Serve feasts at a neighborhood food rack, and eat with them when you're finished serving.
- Provide for a neighborhood good cause.

Those are only a couple of ways you can help. Your own giving is just restricted by your innovativeness. So begin!

Chapter 6

Gratitude

Research has shown appreciation can emphatically affect our lives. It can support our physical and psychological well-being, make us more useful, further develop our independent direction, assist us with controlling our feelings and construct significant connections. All of which can straightforwardly help our monetary prosperity, as well.

Many individuals believe that a speedy and simple way should hoard riches. This is confirmed by the endless monetary items out there that wouldn't exist in the event that there weren't an adequate number of individuals to persuade to get them.

The fact of the matter is your conduct will affect your abundance more than any item. Considering that, it's beneficial to consider the advantages of appreciation and how they can eventually make you a superior steward of your cash - to support yourself and for other people

Concentrations by therapists Robert Emmons and Michael McCullough show that individuals who remembered their good fortune had a more uplifting perspective on life, practiced more, detailed less side effects of disease and were bound to help other people.

This is additionally upheld in work by analyst Nathaniel Lambert that discovers more compelling sensations of appreciation are related with lower realism. Appreciation upgrades individuals' fulfillment with life while diminishing their craving to purchase stuff.

Together they make the establishments for a prosperous future. At the point when you're in a decent spot, you're bound to take part in the good ways of behaving - and keep away from the pessimistic - that can convey that positive sentiment forward. There's a justification for why energy is a typical characteristic among fruitful individuals.

A group of scientists from Northeastern University, the University of California, Riverside, and Harvard Kennedy School found that appreciation can make you more persistent with your cash. Members in the review were given the decision between getting $54 right away or $80 30 days after the fact. The people who were feeling thankful practiced more prominent discretion and were more able to hang tight for higher measures of cash from here on out.

The ramifications for your monetary life are clear. Tolerance and command over one's feelings are essential elements for creating financial wellbeing. Appreciation can be utilized as a device to keep away from hasty monetary decisions and pursue better long haul choices.

Appreciation can likewise emphatically affect our professions, which can prompt different monetary benefits.

As far as one might be concerned, it moves us to be more useful. In one review by clinicians Adam Grant and Francesca Gino, when the supervisor of a raising support call focus offered thanks to representatives for their work, how many calls made by these workers unexpectedly bounced over half the next week.

This ought to surely establish a connection with you in the event that you're a supervisor or organization proprietor.

Offering thanks is likewise a two-way road. Further tests by Grant and Gino have shown the people who helped somebody and afterward got an outflow of appreciation were bound to help again from here on out. Offering gratitude to a predominant, thusly, could be one method for procuring consistent help in propelling your profession and possibly expanding your compensation.

Appreciation basically costs you nothing. Simply your time and exertion. However the advantages are so significant. Offering thanks, whether it is recording everything that you're appreciative for or saying to somebody thank you, can work on your temperament, attitude toward the future, connections, discretion and want to help other people.

It ought to shock no one that the advantages given by appreciation are additionally fundamental fixings to creating financial stability. The more you spend on appreciation today, the more you should be thankful for later on.

At the point when we are more youthful we are educated to utilize "wizardry" words, one of them is "Much obliged". We lose it en route when life happens to us and we start to fail to remember our great habits. Well… .. it is about time we returned to the enchanted word since it makes all the difference. You don't necessarily have all that you need to be appreciative, however you really should be thankful for what you have. Appreciation recognizes that what you have right now may not be precisely the exact thing you need, however it is enough for the present. In my reasoning, appreciation grows the little you assume you have.

We at times neglect to be appreciative for things that regardless of whether we had all the cash on the planet we can't buy, like life, great wellbeing, and family

Celebrating wins both little and enormous is a significant mentality to have this year. As you hold on to win huge, you want to celebrate little wins that keep you moving. We will generally make light of our accomplishments particularly when they appear to be so easy to us, but they really do include at the end of the day. Completing that book you have been attempting to peruse, getting your work-out routine rolling, setting something aside for your just-in-case account, embracing good dieting propensities. Every one of these may appear "little or scheduled" yet for you who are battling you know, they are not excessively little.

So celebrate. Furthermore, as you commend yourself, kindly praise the ones around you for their accomplishments. It will advise them that what they do matters, in the event they neglect it and it will make you a superior individual.

As we start this year let us start with the right attitude, and as you approach vanquishing your monetary world, continue to grin since it looks great on you!

We should audit what appreciation really means for the cerebrum. At the point when you practice appreciation, you support feel-great synthetics like dopamine and serotonin. What's more, appreciation helps in various alternate ways as well. As indicated by an article on Greater Good magazine:

"We tracked down that across the members, when individuals felt more thankful, their cerebrum action was unmistakable from mind movement connected with culpability and the craving to help a reason. All the more explicitly, we found that when individuals who are for the most part more thankful gave more cash to a reason, they showed more noteworthy brain responsiveness in the average prefrontal cortex, a cerebrum region related with learning and navigation. This proposes that individuals who are more thankful are additionally more mindful of how they offer thanks."

As may be obvious, appreciation can advance giving and furthermore supports awareness in the average prefrontal cortex, which influences navigation. Creating financial wellbeing is tied in with using sound judgment with regards to your cash, so appreciation might help.

Abundance is the same amount of mentality as it is numbers, so rehearsing appreciation can get you in the right outlook to really create financial momentum and find a sense of contentment with your relationship with cash.

The beneficial thing about rehearsing appreciation is it is totally free, yet the advantages compound over the long haul and can assist you with building a rich life, money related etc.((for instance, you can be wealthy in wellbeing or love). In the event that you've done nothing like this, you could have a threatened outlook on getting everything rolling. Be that as it may, you don't need to be.

It is really simple and rehearsing gratitude is all exceptionally private. You can be thankful for anything, enormous or little. It doesn't simply need to be huge things like your wellbeing or connections. You can be thankful for a warm mug of espresso, a decent hair day, or a radiant day. There are no set in stone responses!

You can begin by posting three things you're thankful for every day. You can pick morning or night. To assist with causing it to feel all the more genuine and to have the option to follow it, record the three things you're thankful for on a piece of paper.

It will change everyday in view of your work, life, responsibilities, and so on. Keep in mind, you can list anything that you're appreciative for, regardless of how little. The key is to be reliable. As you fabricate consistency, you'll begin to see the advantages.

With regards to your funds, you could be thankful for the cash in your financial records. You could be appreciative of your obligation for assisting you with getting past difficult situations or be thankful you have the cash to take care of your bills. Each of these helps shift your cash attitude.

Beside recording three things you're appreciative for every day, you can compose a card to say thanks to somebody who has helped you. You can verbally show appreciation to your companions, family, and partners. You can likewise work on saying "much obliged" more and taking a stock over the course of the day of what you're appreciative for.

You could think creating financial momentum is about cash, but on the other hand it's a lot about mentality. To develop a cash mentality that assists you with creating financial momentum, appreciation is a key part. Why? Since appreciation can assist with moving your attitude from shortage to overflow, assist you with spending less, and feel significantly improved.

Effectively rehearsing appreciation assists you with acknowledging the amount of you possess to be thankful for right now as opposed to zeroing in on where's going wrong.
A viewpoint that everything is limited spotlights on what's missing and consistently needs more. It seems like there will never be sufficient. This mentality can be destructive to your monetary wellbeing since you can settle on unfortunate choices out of dread.

On the off chance that you have a world view limited by fear you may be modest (and not parsimonious, there is a distinction) or you may very well never pass on that task to go into business. Perhaps you crowd cash as opposed to effective financial planning. Zeroing in on shortage can influence you in various ways.

At the point when you are in an overflow mentality, you understand your chances are boundless. You don't fear contests or believe there will never be sufficient, you think there is in every case all that could possibly be needed. Zeroing in on overflow can assist you with drawing in more cash and have a better cash mentality.

Appreciation can assist with building that overflowing muscle. Suppose that you have a studio condo yet you fantasy about having your own 2-room house. You don't have the vehicle you need presently yet envision getting a Tesla.

At the point when you center around appreciation, you center around the way that you have a rooftop over your head, that you're sound, that your vehicle actually works as opposed to zeroing in on the way that you don't have a 2-room house or Tesla yet.

At the point when you center around appreciation and appreciate and value what you have now, you begin to understand that you really want even short of what you thought. In the present culture, we are molded to need more, to look for far superior, which obviously influences our spending.

Being satisfied with what you have now can prompt less spending since you understand you have all that you really want. That doesn't imply that you can't make progress toward more. It implies that you can partake in the excursion as opposed to feel the torture of where's going wrong.

Appreciation is an incredible asset to change your life and funds and it's thoroughly free. Begin today by posting three things you're thankful for and give it a shot for seven days. You could be astonished at the outcomes.

Ravenousness and dread are two perspectives now and then connected with bringing in cash, speculation choices and establishing long term financial stability procedures.

This Thanksgiving, attempt appreciation for all things considered.

There is a connection among appreciation and more prominent record adjusts, more prominent venture portfolios and more noteworthy fulfillment over spending choices, as per monetary counsels who have seen how cash and feelings blend.

"By rehearsing appreciation, we can conquer the desire to spend on belongings that won't build our satisfaction and spotlight on regions like investing quality energy with loved ones," said James Vermillion of Vermillion Private Wealth in Lexington, Ky.

"Appreciation can likewise assist us with deferring delight and stay away from the motivation for guaranteed compensation as a trade-off for additional beneficial rewards later."

Undoubtedly, many individuals could find it trying to feel monetarily appreciative when such countless parts of Americans' monetary lives presently feel extended meager.

Is a glass half vacant, or half full? The response might show an individual's psychological default to shortage or overflow.

Shortage, genuine or saw, can lead an individual to concentrate strongly — and restlessly — on the inadequacies, concentrating on show. Different examinations show emotional well-being can assume a significant part in shopping propensities; a family where somebody experiences misery has "striking contrasts" in its spending qualities, scientists as of late said.

"An emphasis on appreciation for what we have, joined with good faith and energy about what's to come, removes us from a mentality of shortage and into one of overflow," said Melissa Walsh of Clarity Financial Design in Winter Park, Fla.

Assuming somebody begins with appreciation for what they as of now have, that mentality "can bring down motivation based monetary choices, as costly drive buys, in light of the fact that appreciation can remove us from the quick second and assist us with pulling together in a long haul, values-based direction."

Avarice is the specific inverse of appreciation, as per Corey Voorman of Voorman Investment Counsel in Plymouth, Mich. Not knowing when to tone down venture hazards can be deducted from a portfolio, he noted.

"Voracity frequently accompanies a craving for irrational control, and is frequently bundled with stress which can be harmful for financial backers' profits or assumptions in any market climate," Voorman said. "Appreciation is one of the most mind-blowing weapons against covetousness and dread in effective financial planning."

Appreciation helps set the guide on what occurs next once an individual has gathered enough for themselves, consultants said. All in all, on the off chance that the quest for more abundance isn't the last objective, it opens up somebody's psyche to consider what is.

"Financial independence is more than just having enough money to meet your needs — it's about aligning your values with your financial plan: the peace of mind to focus on the things that matter most, the peace of knowing you can live a life of your choosing, and the peace of planning to care for those you love," said Nicole

Gopoian Wirick, founder of Prosperity Wealth Strategies in Birmingham, Mich.

www.ingramcontent.com/pod-product-compliance
Lightning Source LLC
LaVergne TN
LVHW050320160826
845677LV00014B/3497

* 9 7 9 8 3 5 1 7 9 8 5 8 5 *